Whidbey Island's Special

And the People Who Love Them

By Dan Pedersen

Design by Craig Johnson
Photography by Dan Pedersen except as otherwise noted.

Front cover: Admiralty Inlet and Port Townsend as viewed from Fort Casey.

Back cover: West Beach at Deception Pass State Park.

ISBN-13: 978-0-615-31556-0

Refer inquiries to:
Dan Pedersen
dogwood@whidbey.com
PO Box 1588
Langley, WA 98260

To order signed copies of this book from the author, visit: *www.whidbeywriter.com*

Printed in the beautiful Pacific Northwest, USA, on post-consumer recycled stock, using Earth Ink.

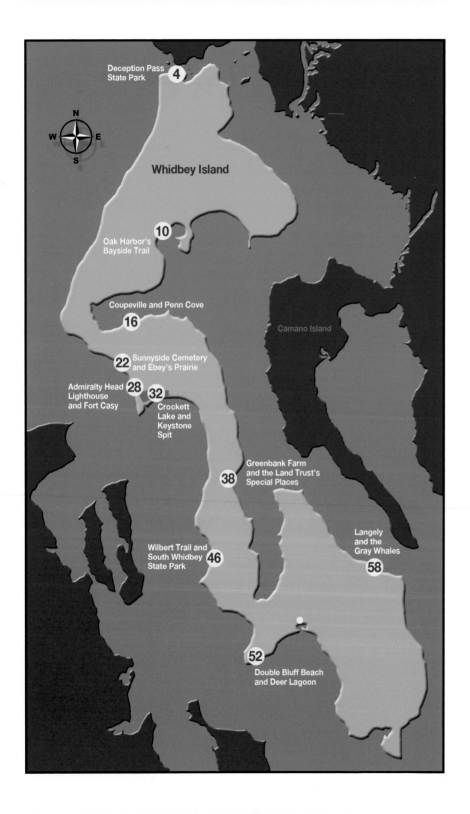

Contents

Introduction

Whidbey Island is a place of forests, farms, prairies and shores — a far cry from the crowded mainland, minutes away by bridge or ferry. People cherish these places for their soothing beauty and diversity. For generations they have brought peace and rejuvenation, and a chance to reflect.

Some are natural areas; others, places where we walk in the footsteps of pioneer ancestors. Island life revolves around rural communities where life is friendly and slow. Publishing a definitive list of the special places is impossible because no two people would agree, but the ones described here are mine, for many reasons.

All are publicly accessible. They are special because people have recognized their value and protected their character for future generations. More are being preserved all the time on private land through the joint efforts of individual property owners and the non-profit Whidbey Camano Land Trust. A few of these are discussed on pages 42-45.

To the extent that we value these places and respect them, Whidbey Island will continue to delight us with wild birds, deer, coyotes, salmon, orcas, gray whales, wildflowers, old-growth forest, charming communities and rich history. Without the vision and selflessness of many individuals, the special places in this book would have fallen long ago to development and exploitation.

A wonderful transformation comes over many people who spend time on Whidbey. They begin to count their wealth not in dollars but in quality of life. They turn their energies toward passing the blessings of this island to those who will follow.

The stories in this book are told by people who see the bigger picture. I hope you enjoy getting to know them and their passion. And then, in whatever way you can, please join them in leaving a richer legacy to future generations.

From North Beach at Deception Pass State Park, visitors enjoy the view of Fidalgo Island (left), Whidbey Island (right) and Deception Pass Bridge.

What's there: Camping, hiking, picnicking, fishing, canoeing, swimming, trails, beach walking, old-growth forest, boat launches, lakes, Native American sites, interpretive signage and programs.

To get there: Follow Highway 20 to Deception Pass Bridge. From the bridge, drive south 1 mile to the main park entrance at traffic light. Or drive north 1 mile from the bridge to additional park facilities at Bowman Bay and Rosario Beach. For other park facilities and saltwater boat launch take Cornet Bay Road, which intersects Highway 20 across from the main park entrance.

Deception Pass State Park

Exploring the island's crown jewel with 'Ranger Rick'

At 480 years old and 200 feet tall, it would be easy to think the signature Douglas firs of Whidbey Island's northern tip are the oldest trees in Deception Pass State Park.

The ancient trees already were two centuries old when the British explorer, Captain George Vancouver, and his ship's master, Joseph Whidbey, discovered the pass in 1792.

But 480 years is not even close to the oldest tree.

Ranger Rick Blank

Ranger Rick Blank points to a short, gnarled fir, growing bush-like beside the park's Sand Dunes Interpretive Trail, which loops for 1.2 miles just south of the Cranberry Lake swimming beach. "This is the oldest tree and the second oldest life in the park," he explains. "This is 860 years. We know this because we cored it once with The Nature Conservancy," referring to the diagnostic process of boring a small sample of wood from the heart of the tree.

Lichen

Blank is leading a tour this morning of seventh graders from Langley Middle School. He directs the kids' attention to a tree nearby. "Do you see the stuff hanging from that tree back there, sort of like witch's hair? It grows all over the Earth and is lichen. It's not quite a plant. Doesn't have real roots. Doesn't have real leaves. Lichen can live between 10,000 and 12,000 years."

This gnarled, 860-year-old Douglas fir in the sand dunes at West Beach is the oldest tree in the park.

Blank's eye lands on an ant trying to do it. "Oh, look," he tells the group of students. "Here's a little ant. Now let's watch how it's doing, but don't crush it, ok?" The ant makes poor headway and the group moves on.

Blank stops in a shallow depression between a beachfront foredune and the gentler secondary dunes on the inland side of the trail. "What do you think happened in this spot 8,000 years ago?"

"Indians," he says. This was a seasonal village site for extended families from the Lummi Tribe, based near today's Bellingham. Every summer they would load the relatives into canoes and travel among seasonal villages in the San Juan Islands, Whidbey Island and other stops in the area. Along the way they would dig camas roots, smoke clams, get salmon and gather foodstuffs they needed for the winters back home.

Still, it boggles the mind that a short, twisted fir could be older than the giants of the forest that visitors pass on their way through the park to Cranberry Lake. It's no wonder the dunes trail is one of Blank's favorite places to talk about this huge, diverse, most heavily-visited treasure of the state park system.

"Why would this tree be older than any other? Let me tell ya it's because of the sand dunes. The last fire went through about 180 years ago. There was always fire in the forest. Nature had its process – volcanoes, lightning. Even the first peoples used to burn a lot. But this tree happened to be in the sand dunes and no fire got to it."

Neither did pests. Over time, termites and black carpenter ants typically take a toll on trees. "If you were an ant would you like to walk all the way across loose sand from that trail, or the forest, to get to this tree? You would walk forever with your little feet, getting across every little grain of sand."

The sand dunes area extends south along the shore from the West Beach parking area.

Whidbey Island's Special Places

"By July and August they'd come to this place. They had a village right here of driftwood longhouses and came to this park for one reason – berries – all of their berries, especially huckleberries and blackberries."

Blank says the native Americans also harvested Oregon grape and salal berries. Nootka roses grew throughout the area. The Indians got vitamin C from the meat of the rose hips and vitamin E from the seeds. He points out a tall Ocean Spray bush, from which they made shafts for arrows and spears. "This is like an ironwood in a way," he explains. "The women would make their cooking racks out of this. It'd be like a metal cooking rack."

The sand dunes support a specialized community of plants and trees. The dunes are here because of the combined effects of volcanically-formed bedrock, glaciers, erosion, wind and marine currents. Blank explains that glaciers from the east carved Deception Pass and left a moraine in the West Beach area, trapping the fresh-water depression that became Cranberry Lake.

The last advance of the Vashon Glacier was about 19,000 years ago. It receded about 12,000 years ago.

"Is it unusual to have fresh water right next to salt water?" he asks. "Yes. Very abnormal."

Sand erodes from steep bluffs several miles south and is carried to this spot by longshore currents. Meanwhile, other strong currents are flowing through Deception Pass and down Rosario Strait. "There's so much power in those currents that everything stops right by that motor home over there," Blank says, pointing to an RV in the parking lot. So the sand accumulates on the beach, creating a lovely west-facing beach for the public. Wind, in turn, blows the sand into dunes along this stretch of shore.

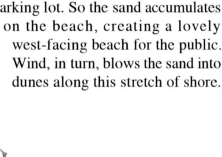

Salal leaves and berries

Old-growth Douglas fir dwarfs vehicles parked at North Beach.

Sand, drift logs and even some tide pools attract visitors to West Beach at Deception Pass State Park. This view looks north toward the opening to Deception Pass. The bridge is out of view, around the corner to the right.

The dune area stretches several hundred feet till it reaches a stand of trees, including the 860-year-old one. The woods stop it from extending further.

Within the dunes, specially adapted plants survive the dry, nutrient-poor environment by staying low, sending roots deep and growing sun-reflective gray, silver and brown foliage. Student work parties have helped clear invasive European dune grass that chokes out everything, to allow smaller clumps of the native grass to come back. In the cleared areas Blank calls attention to Silver Burweed and Morning Glory, currently in bloom, and patches of Yellow Sand Verbena, which attracts the rare Verbena Moth.

Blank has been a ranger for 35 years. Helping visitors understand how nature works is a job he clearly relishes.

"I love it. I am so blessed. If you want to know the best part of my job, this is it right here. It's seeing the light bulbs come on, no matter what the age of the group."

He says outreach is the key to winning public support to protect specialized habitats, birds and animals like those of Deception Pass. "My dream was always for interpretation. Once people understand and see the connections, they appreciate what's here and will possibly even love it. Protecting the resource comes automatically."

And if people will only look, he says, discoveries are all around them.

Seven Bald Eagles live and hunt in the park.

"This is so beautiful. We have this pair of eagles. When I come down here between 4 and 5 a.m. and it's just sorta getting light, you know, little foggy, one of the eagles will be perched on something and the other might be up in those trees there."

Blank says the park is home to seven resident eagles – three adult pairs and one immature bird. Every year the eagles add to their nests, and from time-to-time they move and build a new one.

Some of his favorite eagle encounters have come when he's working between the amphitheater and the trail to North Beach. "I've watched eagles fly right into the tree branches. They'll fold their wings back and hit a dead branch with their breast, break it off, and then catch that branch before it falls to the ground. Then they go and fly to their nest. They nest-build every year."

Blank has a soft spot for owls, too.

"Up in the campground there was this old-growth fir and it blew down two years ago. But gosh it had a nice cavity nest where the Great-horned Owls nested. Ahhhhh! Every night you'd be on patrol and they'd be talking to one another, sitting in their trees."

When a windstorm blew down the tree, Blank said he was afraid the owls would leave. "But you know they just found another tree up behind the camp loop there."

Blank says he came to Deception Pass originally for three reasons. "The rocky Rosario shoreline was my primary reason because I have

always had a vision for an interpretive educational center at Rosario. And we're finally realizing it. Tremendous story. Great native history. So that was number one. The other two reasons were because this is a large park with varied resources and because it had a lot of people coming here. That equaled money to do projects and a chance to tell the story to so many people."

And does Blank have a favorite place at the park?

"You know, I think I do. My favorite place is Bowman Bay on the other side. Maybe it's because I've lived there for 19 years. I just like that you can go there, and, even though there are people all over, find a place to just sit and read or watch."

That may be the real magic of Deception Pass State Park. Even with millions of visitors a year, this exhilarating park still retains extraordinary habitat for wildlife, old growth forest, beauty, peace and solitude to soothe the soul.

Kayakers explore peaceful Cranberry Lake.

What's there: Natural and man-made wetlands, native plants, birds and wildlife, walking, jogging, dog-walking on leash, bird watching. Future site of demonstration rain garden at Scenic Heights trailhead.

To get there: From the traffic light at the main downtown Oak Harbor intersection, where Highway 20 makes a right-angle turn, take Beeksma Drive south to Windjammer Park. From the parking area, walk 100 feet back on Beeksma to intersect the trail west through Freund Marsh to the Scenic Heights trailhead, about one mile. From Windjammer Park the trail also extends eastward along the shore about two miles through Flintstone Park, Old Town, Skagit Valley College, Oak Harbor Marina and across Navy property to Maylor's Point on the far, south side of Oak Harbor Bay.

Oak Harbor's Waterfront Trail

Discovering an urban treasure with environmental educator,
Maribeth Crandell

Red-winged Blackbirds cling to cattails in the peaceful marsh, filling a May afternoon with song. Close by, a female Red-wing holds a choice dragon-fly in her beak, ready to deliver it to hungry nestlings. Savannah Sparrows flit from bush to bush. Hedges of Nootka Rose brighten the trailside with delicate pink blossoms.

Downtown Oak Harbor might seem an unlikely place for so much beauty and bird song. The irony of a wildlife haven within sight of residential neighborhoods and fast-food restaurants isn't lost on Maribeth Crandell, the city's environmental educator. From the Scenic Heights trailhead she points to the far end of this shoreline walk, three miles away on Navy property at Maylor's Point, across from the downtown core.

"You look this way and see Mount Rainier and the bay, and the beautiful marsh and wetland," she says. "Or you look the other way and see rows and rows of condominiums and apartment buildings."

Balancing those two worlds is Oak Harbor's great challenge. On the one hand the city must accommodate the island's highest population density. On the other it must maintain the natural resources and quality of life that drew people here in the first place.

Maribeth Crandell

Left: Commercial buildings are visible from Oak Harbor's waterfont trail as it winds through Freund Marsh.

The trail descends from Scenic Heights, across a footbridge, to the wetlands beyond.

Long ago this historic wetland at the foot of Scenic Heights, on the southwest edge of the city, was drained to create rich agricultural soils for the Freund Farm, which grew a wide variety of crops. Homesteader Ulrich Freund claimed 320 acres here when he stepped ashore in 1851 with Martin Taftzen and Charlie Sumner, two other adventurers who had come up short in the California gold rush. Each took up claims along the shore. Freund's descendants have lived and farmed here ever since.

Historically, this part of the bay was a tidal marsh, Crandell says. "Then it was diked and drained for farmland. Now it is becoming a fresh-water wetland." She pauses and listens to the birdsong. "Nice place for birds! They're used to having people around."

Crandell points out that Freund Marsh is much more than just a place for birds and people. It is where the city directs surface-water runoff from the surrounding uplands so plants and soils can filter it biologically. Runoff flows here in pipes

and drains overland from nearby housing and business communities. In the marsh, it is absorbed by wetland plants and soils that remove many pollutants before the water soaks down into the aquifer or drains to the marine shores. The aquifer supplies drinking water for many islanders. Clean marine shores are important for fishing, shellfish harvesting, swimming and other recreation.

Wetlands are such a good idea that more and more people are creating their own miniature wetlands, called rain gardens, at homes and businesses all over Whidbey Island. At the Scenic Heights trailhead the city plans to build a demonstration rain garden. "A rain garden is just a small, human-made version of a wetland," Crandell says. "You dig a depression. It might be up to three feet deep. Then you put in good, rich, composting soil. Around the edges you put native vegetation or plants that are drought tolerant. Toward the middle, where it will hold water longer, you put wetland plants. The idea is that the water coming off the surrounding hard surfaces such as rooftops, streets, driveways and even some lawns will flow to the rain garden and filter down into the aquifer a little bit more pure than when it came off the paved streets."

A jogger pushes a baby stroller on the Freund Marsh trail.

That's the environmental purpose of a rain garden or wetland such as Freund Marsh. Then there's the human purpose. The trail through the marsh is part of a long-term civic vision to make Oak Harbor's shoreline walkable and accessible for the whole community.

"People need to get out," Crandell says. "It's been proven that people who are depressed benefit from outdoor exercise. In a place like this you aren't closed in on yourself. You get to open up. You get the view and interaction with wildlife and other people walking the dog or pushing the baby stroller. So it feels like a really opening place instead of a place where you're closed in on your own problems.

"Once you get your circulation going, get your muscles working, you get some endorphins going and you just become happier," she says with a laugh as she picks up the pace. "I know people in their 80s and that's what they do – just go for a three-mile walk every day – and they're still doing it. You don't have to be a super athlete. You just take a stroll. It's a way to keep weight off when we have this obesity epidemic in America." She points toward the restaurants and buildings in the distance, adding, "If you look around here in Oak Harbor, you see there is plenty of temptation, plenty of fast food. I know a lot of people who take advantage of it. But you have to counteract that with some good exercise or it's going to do you in," she says.

Right: A male Red-winged Blackbird proclaims his territory.

The bayside trail winds its way east along the shore from Windjammer Park.

Crandell points out the shoreline trail is the perfect place for walking, with its level path and wide view. "You don't feel like somebody's going to sneak up from behind. There are people around. It's not far from the main street. There are houses on one side. It's not a place that feels scary at all. It has clean air, some nice views of wildlife, some lush vegetation, everything you need to encourage people to walk. Being so close to downtown it's convenient for people during their lunch hour. People can just leave their house with the dog and take a walk or push the baby stroller."

Places like Freund Marsh also benefit the economy of Oak Harbor and Puget Sound. "Much of the economics of our area is based on salmon and shellfish. At Penn Cove we have the world's largest commercial mussel farm. Their business cares a great deal about water quality. So do all the people who dig shellfish recreationally. Here in Oak Harbor we have a lot of boats going in and out of our marina to fish for salmon, but where do you go for salmon you feel you can eat safely? Puget Sound is really becoming vulnerable to water quality issues. Getting control of water quality starts with the housing that goes up the hillside and the quality of the storm water that's draining down into the bay."

Crandell pauses on a footbridge over a drainage canal on the marsh and points to an outfall dribbling brownish surface-water runoff into a frothy canal. "Here on this bridge you can see the remnants of our society going downstream."

From Freund Marsh on the west end of the bay, the shoreline trail winds east, then south and west, completing three quarters of a loop. "It runs between the beach and the baseball fields, so families who are watching a little league game can also play with their kids on the beach. Then it goes past some condos and along a paved street, and across the yacht club and marina, onto Navy property out to Maylor's Point, where you're in a wild area again. So you can go for miles along the waterfront."

The trail goes right past the waterfront playground.

Whidbey Island's Special Places

This view looks southeast from Flintstone Park toward Oak Harbor Marina and the Maylor's Point area (at right).

Garry Oaks spread their canopies over the intersection of S.E. Pioneer Way and Regatta Drive.

Along the way, the trail winds through Flintstone Park and past Oak Harbor's Old Town, where remnants of Maylor's Wharf are still visible. The wharf was built in 1893 and burned in 1966, but the concrete pier at its end is still visible offshore, toward Maylor's Point. Garry Oak trees, for which Oak Harbor is named, are prevalent throughout the Old Town and especially in Smith Park, along Midway Boulevard and on Regatta Drive by Skagit Valley College. The remnant of an oak savannah is visible just behind a chain-link fence that separates Skagit Valley College from Navy property just beyond. Such savannahs were once found in dry areas from British Columbia to California. In addition to the oak trees they supported a distinct plant community of native grasses and wildflowers.

For residents and visitors alike, Oak Harbor's bayside trail is truly a treasure hidden in plain sight.

Coupeville Wharf offers a restaurant and shops, moorage, and interpretive displays.

Coupeville and Penn Cove

Remembering the tragic orca captures of the 1970s with Howard Garrett and Susan Berta

It's a Sunday morning in late June and Coupeville is just waking up. On sunny Front Street the first dawdling tourists are lingering by shop windows as a handful of single-minded locals unload tabletop displays, video monitors and literature from their cars.

The displays are headed for the far end of Coupeville Wharf, where the blue waters of Penn Cove lap gently against pilings and floats. This is Wharf Fest weekend, and marine groups are setting up tables and exhibits in the small complex of shops, restaurant and offices at the head of the wharf.

Among them are Howard Garrett and Susan Berta, founders of the Whidbey-based Orca Network, *www.orcanetwork.org*. In this historic cove, Native American culture thrived for thousands of years, and New England seafarers established a town that still shows off 150-year-old architecture. But Garrett and Berta are here to talk about another community that was here before either of those, and still remains.

Susan Berta and Howard Garrett stand on Coupeville Wharf. Behind them is the site of the orca captures of 1970 and 71.

Orcas are fast-swimming and capable of dramatic displays. This one is breaching, perhaps just to look around. ©2009 Dave Ellifrit, Center for Whale Research.

Orcas, or killer whales, have roamed Puget Sound and both sides of Whidbey Island since the glaciers retreated about 10,000 years ago. Social and intuitive, they spend their entire lives with their extended families. They communicate with completely distinct local vocalizations and live more-or-less human spans of 40-90 years. While other populations of orcas are found worldwide, the Southern Resident community is specific to the Salish Sea of northern Puget Sound. They do not interbreed or associate with other orca groups, which occasionally visit these waters. The three pods of Southern Residents keep to themselves, consume mainly Chinook salmon, and range in total population from about 70 to 100 individuals.

But none of this was known in the 1960s and 70s, in the run-up to two of the saddest chapters in the history of man's relationship with orcas. The gut-wrenching events took place in Penn Cove within sight of this wharf, near the Captain Whidbey Inn, in the summers of 1970 and 71.

Garrett, the author of *Orcas in Our Midst*, explains that for several years, marine aquariums had been capturing orcas and putting them on display. Orcas had been considered vicious killers. "In fact it was common for fishermen to go out in their boats and shoot a few if they got the chance.

Whidbey Island's Special Places

And the US and Canadian navies had guns set up to shoot orcas and recommended in their divers' manuals to, 'Kill them if you get a chance. But don't get into the water with them,'cause they'll kill you.'" That prevailing wisdom was entirely false, he says. "They've never harmed a human in the wild."

In the summer of 1970, two Seattle-area entrepreneurs, Don Goldsberry and Ted Griffin, set out to capture some orcas for shipment to aquariums worldwide. Using spotters in aircraft, they located a large group in the Possession Sound area south of Whidbey Island.

"So they sent out the speedboats to herd them into Saratoga Passage, throwing bombs in the water and buzzing them as fast as they could," Garrett says. "The idea was to herd them into Holmes Harbor. But the pursuers already had carried out some earlier captures and the orcas recognized the boat noises and knew exactly what was going to happen, that their young were going to be taken from them."

So the orcas made a desperate bid to save their babies.

"Knowing what was going on, the females with their calves dove and swam north, heading no doubt for Deception Pass to get away," Garrett says. "All the rest, the males, stayed on the surface and went east into Port Susan. They were the decoys and diverted the speedboats into Port Susan. But of course the females with the young eventually had to come up, and when

Orcas remain together in their family groups. © 2009 Howard Garrett

An orca calf swims close behind its mother. © 2009 Dave Ellifrit, Center for Whale Research.

they did, somewhere between Holmes Harbor and Penn Cove, the aircraft spotted them and the boats got into position."

The boats caught up with them at Penn Cove, turned them into the bay and drove them all the way to the end, where they cornered them and deployed nets from shore-to-shore.

"Right away all the males and adults showed up," Garrett says. "So the capture team put another net around the males, thinking there might be some babies in that group, too. But they didn't have to because those orcas absolutely would not leave, would not go anywhere, while their families were trapped. So they had them all. Ted Griffin estimated 96 at the time."

Garrett says he watched recently-found TV footage that shows six or eight divers yanking on ropes wrapped around the young orcas, "pulling them over to get a net around them, a sling under them, to get them onto the flatbed truck. It's horrendous to watch. You can hear the anguished wails, the wails of the orcas," being separated from their young.

A riot of colorful flowers adds to the charm of Coupeville's Front Street.

Many orcas died that day, and in a second capture carried out in Penn Cove a year later. Most of the captured orcas died within a few years of going on display in marine aquariums, and the operation took out an entire 10-year age group of reproductive females. But the public was gradually learning, and several of the captured animals survived long enough to inspire a popular movement for their protection. By 1976, a court ruling stopped Goldsberry and Griffin from further captures in the state.

One orca that taught the world a great deal was Namu, captured accidentally by fishermen in British Columbia in 1965 and displayed at the Seattle Aquarium until his death about a year later. "Namu showed us that far from being vicious, Orcas are companions and build relationships," Garrett says. "They carry out trust exercises." Garrett says aquarium owner, Ted Griffin, would sit by the tank and Namu would come up and put his jaws around Griffin's foot. "At first, of course, Ted would yank his foot back in fear, but Namu would come up again and do it until Ted got the idea. He'd just sort of rest his teeth on Ted's foot. It was a way of saying, 'Of course I could, but I'm not going to.' It was a way to let Ted know, 'You can trust me.'"

Garrett says trainers in marine parks all over the country tell a consistent story. "Orcas are not just easy to train but eager to learn. Trainers barely have to describe what they want and they'll do it. You just basically suggest and they understand and want to cooperate. That's how social they are."

It would be safe to say orca education is Garrett's life. He traces the turning point to 1981, when he moved to Washington to help his brother, Ken Balcomb, at the Whale Museum in Friday Harbor. Scholarly research on orcas was accumulating but was not reaching the general public. Garrett took up that challenge. By the 1990s a popular movement was growing to free the whale Keiko, featured in the motion picture, Free Willy. "We realized right away that we had a better candidate in Lolita, who was captured right here in Penn Cove and survives to this day in Miami," Garrett says. So Garrett started his nonprofit, Free Lolita campaign.

"In short order I met Susan Berta, who was running the Beach Watchers program in Island County. I came in and gave some talks to the group. Susan wanted to help, so we joined forces right then," he says.

Together, Garrett and Berta launched an ingenious project, The Orca Network, which engages thousands of Puget Sound residents in reporting orca sightings to a central database. The wide network of spotters enables Garrett and Berta to track the orcas' whereabouts, monitor individuals by their distinctive dorsal fin and saddle patch markings, and detect births and deaths. In a population of fewer than 100, every change is important. The many people who report sightings to The Orca Network also learn about these creatures and, in the process, become advocates for them.

By the 1990s Garrett says it was obvious the Southern Resident Orcas were struggling as salmon stocks collapsed in Puget Sound and in rivers the length of the West Coast. "We realized our focus had to broaden from just bringing Lolita home to taking care of her family. That means looking at the entire issue of habitat. If we are going to take care of these whales we've got to look upstream at habitat in Idaho and Montana, and for that matter, all up and down the coast." The orcas need salmon, Garrett explains, and the salmon need healthy habitat.

'Lady Washington' brings maritime history to life on a summer visit to Penn Cove.

Looking out at the tranquil waters of Penn Cove from Coupeville Wharf, it is hard to sense trouble. These abundant and sheltered shores have nurtured human communities for generations. But the calm waters conceal a deeper story. For now, people and orcas still live side-by-side, in a fragile balance, as they have done for thousands of years. Throughout the island and Puget Sound, probably no other creature in the wild inspires such outright awe.

If humans are at the top of the food-chain among creatures of the land, then the same may also be said of orcas among creatures of the sea. Penn Cove remains one of the best places of all to reflect on that and appreciate how closely our two futures are linked by the need for clean marine waters and safe, abundant food.

The Ferry House at Ebey's Landing is where early travelers waited for the boat to Port Townsend

Sunnyside Cemetery and Ebey's Prairie

Walking in the pioneers' footsteps, with historian Roger Sherman

"Sometimes I get choked up when I talk about this one," Roger Sherman admits as he pauses at a short gravestone nestled among larger monuments.

"It's sad. This kid was…he was Isaac Ebey's grandson, Edward, just three years old." Sherman points to the carved stone of a bird lying dead on its back. "This is a fallen dove," he explains with a hitch in his voice. "It's a dove with a little cross behind it."

Edward Ebey tombstone

Roger Sherman

Sherman, a retired farmer and ship's captain, is also a maritime historian, author and cemetery district commissioner. From his hillside home on Sherman Road, west of Coupeville, he looks across fields that once were part of the 1850 Donation Land Act claim of Isaac Ebey, the first homesteader on Whidbey Island. Portions of the land later became part of Sherman Farms, where Sherman's family raised turkeys and dairy cattle.

Ebey settled 640 acres of the richest land on central Whidbey and farmed it till 1857, when he was beheaded by a raiding party of northern Kake Indians. "His wife, Rebecca, is right here," Sherman points out. "She lasted only two years – comes out on the Oregon Trail and then dies two years later. Her mother died on the trail."

Tombstones mark the final resting place of many members of the Ebey family at Sunnyside Cemetery.

Pioneer life took a brutal toll of children and young adults. "Rebecca, in the two years she was here, had a daughter, Sarah, and Sarah died when she was seven. They lost a lot of kids in those days – didn't have the antibiotics. And of course tuberculosis was the one that got a lot of them.

"Yeah," Sherman sighs, "lots of sadness."

For Sherman, the cemetery's oldest section reflects the history of central Whidbey one life at a time. His affection for each one is clear. "They were all people and they all had stories."

The Davis Blockhouse, on the grounds of today's Sunnyside Cemetery, was built in 1857 to help defend the donation land claim of James Davis. He was one of three brothers of Rebecca Davis Ebey.

Sherman's interest in those stories really started a few years ago when he was writing a book on central Whidbey's maritime history. From the 1850s -80s Penn Cove attracted a great many seafarers, starting with Captain Thomas Coupe, for whom Coupeville is named. Much of the early shipping was of logs and lumber bound for California and ports worldwide. Later, in the decades before the 1935 opening of Deception Pass Bridge, the island was served by schooners and steamships that carried passengers, farm produce, mail and freight throughout Puget Sound.

"All the old sea captains, you know, are up here," Sherman explains. After he became a cemetery commissioner and started learning more, he said it just seemed like the pioneers' stories ought to be shared. So in partnership with the county historical society he started giving cemetery tours to the public several times each summer.

In 1998 Sherman published *The Sinking of the Calista, Part 1 of A Maritime History of Central Whidbey Island.* "Here's Calista right here – Calista Lovejoy," he points out. "The steamer was named for her." The beautiful passenger-and-cargo ship was built in 1911 and sunk in 1922 after a collision in the fog with a freighter near Seattle. Five of Sherman's relatives were among 75 passengers aboard, but all survived and were rescued. Sherman built the den of his home to replicate the passenger cabin, with port holes and arching beams. "I always tell the story of Calista. It's one of those cases where a 17-year-old married an absent sea captain about 20 years older. So guess what? He dies and leaves her with six kids to raise."

The young widow took another husband, but his story is lost. "The guy she remarried, name of Leach, there's no record of him in the cemetery. Yet Calista is buried back here with the father of her children."

Sherman picks up the story of the Ebeys.

"Isaac talked his whole family into coming out – his siblings and parents. They came out in 1854 and took the homestead up on top of the hill, adjoining Isaac Ebey's, and called it Sunnyside Farm," Sherman explains. "That's where the name of the cemetery came from." Their daughter, Mary, inherited the land when her parents died and donated a portion for an extended-family Ebey gravesite and cemetery.

The Jacob Ebey Blockhouse stands next to the home of Jacob and Rebecca Ebey. It was one of four blockhouses that surrounded the house.

Jacob and Sarah Ebey built a saltbox house that has been preserved by the National Park Service and is occasionally opened to the public for community historical events.

Jacob Ebey was a colonel in the Army and had served in the War of 1812, the Black Hawk War of 1832 and the Mexican War of 1846. "In the Black Hawk War he fought with Abraham Lincoln," Sherman points out. "You don't hear much about that. They were friends."

After Jacob Ebey arrived on Whidbey he built four blockhouses for defense from any hostile raiders, one near each corner of his house, with the resolve of a battle-tested military officer. One of the blockhouses, later rebuilt from the ground up, remains standing beside the Jacob Ebey house today. "Then he built a 12-foot high stockade between the blockhouses, with pointy ends and the whole bit. You know he was ready," Sherman laughs.

Finding new ways to tell the pioneers' stories has led to some magical moments for the community, Sherman says. "One thing we did that was a lot of fun, but an awful lot of work, was hold a reenactment. We had many of the pioneers come alive, using actors from the high school drama club and the history day committee. We had them in period costume. Docents would lead groups around to the different gravesites and the person there would recite two or three minutes' worth of their life. It was a great attraction and I wish we could do it again, but as I said, it was an awful lot of work!"

Today, reminders of the pioneers can be found all over central Whidbey. The island's history was shaped not only by European and American settlers but by Chinese immigrants who did much of the farm labor.

The Jacob Ebey house, built in 1855, was getting a new roof and siding in 2008. At the time of this writing it is open to the public only during special events.

Members of Sherman's family have recovered used opium vials and ginger beer flasks from forgotten dump sites in their fields where Chinese migrant farm laborers disposed of them around the turn of the century. The smuggling of Chinese, in violation of the Chinese Exclusion Act of 1882, was big business for a time.

On Ebey's Landing Road, just up from the beach, is a weathered old house built in 1860 by Isaac Ebey's two sons, Eason and Ellison. Sherman's great grandfather, Francis LeSourd, remembered it as The Ebey Inn. Today it is called The Ferry House. "It was kind of a hotel or bed and breakfast," Sherman said.

A schooner, known as the ferry, crossed once a day with passengers and freight from Port Townsend to the beach at Ebey's Landing. "If you missed the boat you had to stay at the inn overnight." In those days Port Townsend, on the far shore of Admiralty Inlet, was the nearest real civilization. "So everything and everyone came through Port Townsend. If someone wanted to get to Whidbey they would come across from Port Townsend to Ebey's Landing."

The coastline at Ebey's Landing is one of the prettiest and most photographed spots on the west side of Whidbey Island. A popular hiking trail ascends from a parking area at the foot of the bluff and follows the rim for nearly two miles west. The trail offers spectacular views of farm fields and marine waters.

Because of the landing's exposure to west winds and the open ocean no dock was ever built. The ferry could not land on the beach. Instead, it sent passengers ashore in small boats. Livestock often were pushed overboard to swim ashore from a barge the ferry sometimes towed.

Today, most of Ebey's Prairie is permanently preserved as agricultural land within the Ebey's Landing National Historical Reserve. Whidbey Camano Land Trust is working with the reserve to expand protection to still more adjoining parcels. It is impossible to look upon the green and golden fields, black earth and open expanse of this landscape without feeling a profound sense of peace.

Visitors to Sunnyside Cemetery and Ebey's Prairie may wish to begin their journey on the cemetery's website, *www.sunnysidecemetery.org.* There they will find a rich account of central Whidbey and the pioneers buried at the cemetery, written by historian Theresa Trebon.

What's there: Lighthouse and fortifications. High bluff views, trails, historical site, kite flying, picnicking, beach-walking, deer, wild birds and wildflowers. Gift shop and historical displays inside lighthouse, open to the public on a seasonal schedule.

To get there: From the traffic signal at Highway 20 in Coupeville, turn west on Main Street, which becomes Engle Road. Continue 3.5 miles past the Camp Casey offciers' quarters, lawns and barracks to the entrance of Fort Casey State Park on right. Enter the park and follow signs to parking areas for either the lighthouse or concrete fortifications. Both are within easy walking distance of each other.

Admiralty Head Lighthouse and Fort Casey

Going back a century with lighthouse docent, Dick Malone

"These were called disappearing guns," Dick Malone explains. "From the water you couldn't see them. They were down below this wall."

The busload of third-graders converges on Malone, hanging on every word. "The gun goes up and fires. Then it comes back down behind the wall. When it goes below the wall it's invisible."

The barrel of the big gun weighed 35 tons, he explains. "So how do you suppose they made that thing go up and down?"

"Um…it might have been the shock of the bullet going out," a youngster suggests. "Exactly!" Malone replies. "It's called recoil." He explains that when the gun was fired, the kick pushed it backwards, pivoting down to a lower position, concealed behind the wall. As the gun swung down it lifted a 55-ton lead counterbalance that would be locked in the up position till it was time to raise the gun for the next shot. To raise the gun, the soldiers would release the weight and let it descend. "Like a teeter-totter," he tells the kids.

Dick Malone tells third-graders about Fort Casey's big guns.

This 10-inch gun at Fort Casey is locked in the upright firing position. Nearby, another gun is displayed in the concealed position, behind the wall.

Fort Casey was built in the late 1890s as a coastal defense installation and used till the end of World War II. It had seven of the big 10-inch guns. Each could fire a 617-pound shell about eight miles across the narrow entrance of Admiralty Inlet. Hostile ships entering Puget Sound would have to run the gauntlet between this fort and two others on the opposite shore, which covered a zone called the triangle of fire. None ever tried.

Malone is a volunteer docent at Admiralty Head Lighthouse. He loves sharing the story of Fort Casey's guns and what it was like to live in the nearby lighthouse a century ago. Whether he's speaking to school kids, tourists or senior citizens, this retired Marine Corps lieutenant colonel and teacher from Illinois skillfully engages them with questions of his own.

"I had a group once of about 15 or 20 fifth graders," he said. "Another totally separate boy and his grandmother kinda latched onto us. I don't mind that. After about 15 minutes I usually ask the kids some questions

to see what they know. Pretty soon this youngster, obviously smaller than the 5th graders, started to answer my questions and he was right most of the time." So during a break between groups Malone asked the grandma how old the boy was, only to learn he was just finishing first grade. "'The way he was answering questions I wouldn't have guessed that,'" Malone told her. "'Yeah,' she said, 'he just loves to watch the History Channel with grandpa.'"

Long before there was a fort here, this lonely headland was the site of Puget Sound's first lighthouse, originally housed in a wood frame building. The light was lit in 1861. Whale oil kept the flame burning and a Fresnel lens of precisely-focused prisms concentrated the flame into a beacon visible for up to 16 miles offshore.

"Our light didn't blink," Malone says. "It didn't need to because it was the first." When additional lighthouses later became active on Puget Sound each had a unique signature – a combination of flashes, pauses and sometimes colors – so mariners would know which light they were seeing. Admiralty Head projected a solid white light with no pauses.

Visitors explore the main batteries at Fort Casey.

The ships coming and going from Puget Sound in the late 1800s relied on sails and wind. At night the shore was pitch dark, and clouds often prevented mariners from using the stars to navigate. Zig-zagging with the wind but surrounded on all sides by islands and mainland, the ships' captains needed to know their exact position. The early lighthouses helped them operate safely.

After construction started on Ft. Casey, Admiralty Head Lighthouse was relocated nearby to make room for the guns, and the original wood-frame lighthouse eventually was torn down. The Fresnel lens was moved in 1903 into the gleaming new brick-and-stucco lighthouse that still stands today and captures the imagination of thousands of visitors a year.

By the 1920s most vessels were powered by steam, and in 1922 the lighthouse was decommissioned. But for decades leading up to that time, life at the lighthouse was mostly lonely and filled with hours of work, polishing and cleaning the oil lamp, maintaining the building and tending livestock and gardens. The light keeper was appointed by the President of the United States and was often a bachelor military man, though some were married and brought wives and children to share the unusual lifestyle. The keeper's appointment was considered a reward for service to the country in the military or merchant marine.

Work is ongoing today to improve the lighthouse's historical displays, led by Washington State University Lighthouse Docents. The nonprofit group staffs the building and keeps its doors open to the public in a cooperative agreement with the owner, Washington State Parks and Recreation Commission.

When Dick Malone is not leading tours he can often be found in his workshop at home. One of his contributions to the lighthouse was an exquisite oak-topped workbench for the tower room, which he created to specifications found in the building's original blueprints. Also on display is a replica Malone built of a U.S. Lighthouse Service traveling library. This is a small upright bookcase with twin doors that held an assortment of books and magazines to help light keepers and their families pass the hours, weeks and months of solitude. Every few months a ship would visit from the lighthouse service, bringing fresh supplies and a new traveling library and taking the old one away.

Through the efforts of many individuals and organizations, visitors today can stand at this commanding spot on a high bluff overlooking Admiralty Inlet and experience a sense of what life was like generations ago for the light keepers and soldiers who served on Whidbey Island.

Traveling libraries like this one circulated books to the lighthouse keepers.

Dunlin congregate at Crockett Lake on a quiet November day. ©2009 Craig Johnson

Crockett Lake and Keystone Spit

Photographing birds with Craig and Joy Johnson

"We're going to do something crazy here, but no one's coming and we've got a second," Craig Johnson says as he steers his Subaru Outback into the oncoming lane and opens the sunroof.

He is scanning the marsh. At his right is a friend who's a novice bird photographer, and sitting in back is Joy Johnson, peering through binoculars and scribbling in her journal. They've just passed several Red-winged Blackbirds on the cattails and a Great Blue Heron in a drainage canal, so close that the beginner can't zoom back enough to get the whole bird in his viewfinder.

"Here's what we're going to do," Johnson says. "I'll stop and back up slowly. You aim your camera out the sunroof and see if you can get that Red-tailed Hawk," he suggests, pointing out a juvenile Red-tail on a utility pole behind them. The beginner had overlooked it while watching the roadside.

Craig and Joy Johnson

The friend's camera is a Canon 40D digital single lens reflex with 100-400 image stabilized zoom lens. It's handheld equipment, just enough telephoto to do this. It is similar in capabilities to the Nikon that Johnson used to photograph three books of Puget Sound birds. Except that Johnson has an uncanny gift for getting close.

Adult Red-tailed Hawk
© 2009 Craig Johnson

The passenger is twisting in his seat, looking up through the sunroof and asking Johnson if he can back up some more.

"Too late," Johnson says. "He's gone. Happens all the time – don't feel bad," as he veers back into his lane. "Keep an eye on this next stretch by the gravel ponds. There! Do you see them lying down right on that rocky spit – Killdeer! Whole bunch of them. They look like rocks," he says, stopping in the road and powering down the window.

"Rest your camera on the rim of the glass and see if you can get a few snaps. I'll turn off the engine to get rid of that vibration."

Johnson is driving the stretch of Highway 20 that wraps around Crockett Lake, one of five Important Bird Areas in Island County designated in 2001 by Audubon Washington. It is one of a handful of Habitats of Local Importance (HOLIs) declared in the county's Critical Areas Ordinance.

This shallow, brackish lake and adjacent Keystone Jetty are a major staging area for 17 species of shorebirds during the autumn migration. During the breeding season this is a favored foraging site for Great Blue Herons. Bald Eagles and nine species of ducks winter here. Falcons, Merlins and Northern Harriers are frequently seen, and in 1999 Whidbey Audubon Society counted 500 Least Sandpipers here, the largest concentration ever recorded in the state. Altogether the local chapter has documented 213 species using the site.

The birds come here for the wide open spaces, relatively light human interference and rich mixture of food sources and habitat. Adjacent to a marine beach, Crockett Lake is mostly open water under estuarine influence. Water flows into Crockett Lake from a large upland area and drains out through a tide-gate. The level fluctuates seasonally and, at times, large areas of mudflats are exposed.

A Greater Yellowlegs forages in the shallows of Crockett Lake. © 2009 Craig Johnson

This and Keystone Spit, and nearby Fort Casey, are favored photography locations for the Johnsons. But birding takes a sharp eye and many people never know what they're missing.

It would be easy on any given day to think no birds are present. But they usually are if one is patient and looks carefully. A good outing is one that results in one or two great photo opportunities, which can be unpredictable and almost anything – such as a coyote instead of a bird.

Coyote was an unexpected bonus at Crockett Lake. © 2009 Craig Johnson

Short-eared Owls perch on pilings and fence posts at Crockett Lake. © 2009 Craig Johnson

"We've done a lot of photography at the fort and in the woods near the lighthouse," Craig Johnson explains. "We often see a Great Horned Owl we named Teddy. Owls are territorial so we look for him whenever we come here, and time after time we see him in the same tree, about 30 feet up. Several times we've seen both adults with the two fledgling owls – all four owls right together in that one tree.

"I wish we could share the thrill of these large birds with everyone we meet at the park, but this is where the birds live and I'm not sure how much attention they can tolerate at one time. We keep a respectful distance, don't make any sudden moves, and do not linger long." People often are tempted to approach a bird until it feels compelled to take flight and leave, but Johnson's idea of a successful shoot is just the opposite. He wants to get his picture and walk away before the bird decides to leave.

"I was talking with a ranger who said, ironically, that most park visitors never even think about the birds and never pause to look up or wonder what they are doing. But the birds are here. This is their home and we need to care for natural areas like this so they will always have a home here."

A Hooded Merganser swims near the lake's flood gate. © 2000 Craig Johnson

Pigeon Guillemots, with red feet, fish near the old pier by the ferry harbor. © 2009 Craig Johnson.

"The phone rings and this guy says, 'We just moved here and we plan to publish a book about birds. Could we meet you for coffee?'" Wood said. "And I'm thinking, 'Yeah right. How many times have I heard that?' But I met them and within several minutes I realized, 'These people are for real.'"

Three books later, Johnson is conservation co-chair of Whidbey Audubon. When he's not producing commercial art of marine vessels for a living he is painting watercolor prints and cards of his favorite birds to sell in local bookstores and wild bird shops. And he is writing letters to elected leaders, advocating for the protection of local wild bird habitat from unnecessary destruction and development. The mission behind all the Johnsons' books, watercolors and website is to educate about birds and inspire others to appreciate and protect birds and their habitat.

For the Johnsons, birding started as a hobby that grew into an obsession. "We just wanted to identify the birds that were coming into our yard so I started photographing them," Craig Johnson says. "Then one day we thought, what are we going to do with all these photographs? Maybe we could make a book."

Belted Kingfisher
© 2009 Craig Johnson

It isn't as far-fetched as it sounds because in addition to being a photographer, Craig Johnson is a skilled graphic designer and a former service representative in the commercial printing industry, and Joy Johnson is a writer.

The Johnsons were just moving to Whidbey from Edmonds and thought it would be a good idea to hook up with the local Audubon chapter, so they placed a call to Frances Wood, who at that time was president of the Whidbey group. She picks up the story:

Rinocerous Aucklet hunts small fish in the afternoon, just off the beach at Keystone. © 2009 Craig Johnson

Like many islanders, the Johnsons visit Crockett Lake and Keystone Spit often. They are drawn by the constantly shifting bird populations, the frequent surprises, and the never failing beauty of this soothing landscape where fields and woods come down to meet the sea.

Our Puget Sound Birds and Habitat, by Craig and Joy Johnson, is available from many Puget Sound area bookstores and wild bird shops. Visit the Johnsons' website at: *www.pugetsoundbackyardbirds.com*.

Least Sandpiper blends into the cobble. © 2009 Craig Johnson.

Bald Eagles keep watch from driftwood perches along the beach. © 2009 Craig Johnson

Pacific Loon was a surprise on a photo outing to Keystone Spit. © 2009 Craig Johnson

What's there: Historic, 151-acre farm with public trails for hiking and dog walking, bird watching, wetlands, WSU Master Gardeners' educational garden, café, wine shop, retail shops, barn space for events, Sunday Farmer's Market, community festivals. Fields offer mountain and marine views to both east and west. Trails extend into county-owned forest and woodland loop. Entire protected area 522 acres.

To get there: From Coupeville, follow Highway 525 south about 10 miles to Wonn Road. Turn east on Wonn Road into farm. From Clinton, follow Highway 525 north about 14 miles to Wonn Road.

Greenbank Farm
and the Land Trust's Special Places
Taking stock of our legacy with Pat Powell
of Whidbey Camano Land Trust

Pat Powell explores the shade garden.

When Pat Powell walks the rolling hills of Greenbank Farm, she is constantly scanning the fields for movement.

"I'm always looking for the coyotes," she says. "We hear them at night and they're quite vocal, but they're still hunted in the county woods and tend to be shy."

Powell lives an easy walk from the farm and gets out on its trails several times a week with her two Corgis. The farm welcomes dog owners if they pick up after their pets. Powell also works right here, in one of the farm's office buildings, as executive director of Whidbey Camano Land Trust, *www.wclt.org*. The wide open landscape is a good place to unwind and think. But not about work.

"No, I almost never think about work," she says. "I try to stay in the present. It's so beautiful out here. I'm always looking at the mountains and fields, sky and clouds, and listening to all these birds," she says, gesturing around. "When you get on the high ground you can look to the west and see the Olympic Mountains and Port Townsend, and then look to the east and see the Cascades and Holmes Harbor. You're right on that dividing line."

Geese, crows and Red-winged Blackbirds have something to say this morning. "In the fields we see a lot of Northern Harriers, Bald Eagles and Great Blue Herons. There's a lot of wildlife here."

Left: This view across the pond at Greenbank Farm looks toward the educational garden of the WSU Master Gardeners.

Greenbank Farm offers acres of fields with trails for hiking and dog walking. The county-owned forest in the distance offers additional trails and a woodland loop.

And that seems appropriate because protecting wildlife habitat is a big part of what drives Powell's work and inspires Land Trust members and community movements like the one a decade ago that saved Greenbank Farm from becoming a massive housing development.

Established in 1904, the farm for years was a dairy operation, but evolved over time and really made its name in the 1970s as the largest Loganberry farm in the United States. Then in 1995 Chateau Ste. Michelle winery announced plans to sell it for a 700-home residential development. The community intervened. "It was a real show of community love," Powell says. At the time she was working for The Nature Conservancy, which purchased a piece of adjacent property by Lake Hancock as part of the larger deal to save the farm. "Island County, the Port of Coupeville and The Nature Conservancy all got together," she says. "The whole deal actually was put together by the Trust for Public Land and they haven't gotten enough credit for what they did."

Resident waterfowl.

Island County advanced the money to buy the farm and the adjoining woods. The Port of Coupeville agreed to purchase the farm and repay the county over time. The port, Greenbank Farm Management Group and Land Trust are working to put a conservation easement on it to protect the farm and keep it open to the public.

"What ties everyone together is wildlife habitat," Powell says. "When you talk to people, they want to protect habitat because they realize we're pushing the wildlife out as we develop. Part of what makes Whidbey Island so incredible is all the coyotes and birds and deer. You see wildlife wherever you go, and habitat is the key to that. If you're going to have wildlife you've got to protect the diversity, including the farm fields, which provide habitat for raptors and all kinds of winter birds."

WSU Master Gardeners' educational garden.

The main barn.

Today, Powell is headed not for the fields but for a different part of the farm, the WSU Master Gardeners educational area south of the duck pond. "This is one corner I never get to," she says, delighting in the explosion of color. "Look at those yellow roses! I always head the other way because my house is over there. And when I walk the dogs it's also that way."

Powell settles into a rustic, stick chair in a shady corner.

"Is that somebody singing?" she asks, leaning to hear. "I think it is. That's what I love about this place!" It's a quiet summer Friday and someone is singing in the garden.

Harry Case (right) and his grandson, Shawn Connor, walk their 176-acre forest.

The Land Trust's Special Places

Forest owner, Harry Case, said it well. "If we are going to save the environment, little people are going to have to do something." Horrified by the devastation of a forest clear-cut he encountered as a young man, he vowed he would obtain a piece of land and log it the right way, with respect for the wildlife and forest health.

So in 1946, Case bought a 176-acre forest on south Whidbey Island and, for six decades, harvested trees sparingly and selectively, always preserving forest succession and diversity. Then in 2008 he signed away the development rights to Whidbey Camano Land Trust. The agreement assures that Case's family may continue to draw a living from this working forest, but it won't ever be leveled and carved into 34 home sites.

Case's feelings for the land reflect the sentiment Pat Powell hears often, in various forms, from the hundreds of landowners and community supporters drawn to the mission of Whidbey Camano Land Trust.

"What motivates them is a love affair with the land," she says. "They are tied to it. They have certain ideals and values that aren't always present in the next generation. We provide a way to keep that love going."

For more than 25 years, the Land Trust has partnered with willing landowners and supporters to save and steward some of the island's highest-quality remaining wildlife habitat, working farms, forests and shorelines. In some cases the owners are in a position to donate conservation easements. In others, the land represents their retirement nest egg, and the Land Trust arranges funding to carry out the transaction.

"These people are so humble," she says. "It's never about them. It's always about the land and the obligation they feel to take care of it. As people get older, many start to worry about their land. They want to make sure that what they've been doing, stewarding this land for future generations, is carried on long after they're gone."

Powell points out that not only are these lands being saved, but in many cases access is being arranged so the public may enjoy them for hiking, bird watching, photography, views and nature appreciation. This is a generous gesture because many of the properties remain in private ownership. "We look at every property and decide what the primary conservation values are, and also look to see if there is some way we can provide reasonable public access."

Bird watchers appreciate the protection of wildlife habitat.

Ebey's Landing National Historical Reserve is a good example, where the Land Trust is obtaining conservation easements to protect many additional parcels of farmland. "Every one of those includes a trail easement in a specified area to be developed in the future in partnership with the landowner, so we won't unduly affect their farm operation. The idea is to create a series of connected trails throughout the reserve – through the farm fields and the forests – connecting to the Kettles Trails and from Fort Casey to Fort Ebey."

Since the Land Trust's formation in 1984, it has protected dozens of properties. Every one is a jewel in its own way. For more information please visit the Land Trust website, *www.wclt.org*. Among the lands that will forever enhance the island's beauty and habitat are:

Boose Conservation Easement. 10 acres on south Whidbey Island, protected solely for wildlife habitat, environmental and scenic values. Donated by Dale and Joani Boose.

Ebey's Reserve Conservation Easements. 250 acres in five conservation easements purchased by the Land Trust with local, state and federal grants to protect working farmland with scenic vistas, aquifer recharge and wildlife habitat.

Strawberry Point. 16 acres east of Oak Harbor, donated by Sally Ann Foote and Martin Chamberlain. Scenic waterfront, critical nearshore fish habitat, mature forest, wildlife habitat.

Northern Harrier surveys the fields of Ebey's Reserve.
© 2009 Craig Johnson

Ebey's Reserve conservation easements extend protection to many hundreds of acres of working farmland. ©2009 Mark Sheehan

Crockett Lake protected area includes 40 acres donated to the Land Trust plus 20 acres sold to Washington State Parks. ©2009 Mark Sheehan.

Crockett Lake. 40 acres donated to Land Trust plus 20 acres sold to Washington State Parks by Gene and Janet Zema. Critical feeding grounds for migratory waterbirds. Scenic vistas and wildlife habitat. Located within Ebey's Reserve.

Del Fairfax Forest Preserve. 50 acres on north Whidbey donated by Dr. George Fairfax. Wildlife habitat, walking trails, seasonal wetland, open space.

Dugualla Flats. 39 acres next to Dugualla Lake, purchased by Land Trust with an Island County Conservation Futures grant and Land Trust funds to protect open space, water quality and wildlife habitat. Includes wetlands and streams. Future use for education and bird watching.

Hammons Preserve. 9.5 acres on south Whidbey Island, from the estate of Alvin Hammons. Wildlife habitat, wetland and stream, public access and trail, heritage orchard.

Harry's Forest Forever Conservation Easement. 176-acre working forest northwest of Langley. Easement donated by Harry Case. Wildlife habitat, intact forest community, watershed protection and future trails.

Hayes Conservation Easement. 90 acres northeast of Oak Harbor, donated by three property owners who wanted to be sure the agricultural resources, natural features and scenic rural landscapes on these properties would be protected forever.

Heath Conservation Easement. 90 acres along Admiralty Inlet on central Whidbey Island. The Land Trust helped the original landowner, Albert Heath, preserve a view corridor on the popular Ebey's Landing Bluff Trail by creating a setback for future home building. This conservation easement ensures that homes do not intrude into the scenic hiking experience while walking the bluff trail in Ebey's Reserve.

Hoypus Addition. 52 acres added to Deception Pass State Park. With grants and donations, the Land Trust facilitated the park's purchase of this undeveloped forest land next to the park's Hoypus unit. It helps protect the park's old growth stands and allows loop-trail opportunities for non-motorized users such as equestrians, hikers and cyclists.

Krueger Farm. 4.5 acres at Coupeville, purchased by the community and now owned by the town, alongside an additional 12.5 acres donated by the landowner. The Land Trust holds a conservation easement, ensuring permanent protection of open space, trail access and wildlife habitat for future generations.

Libbey Beach tidelands. 1,200 feet of tidelands purchased by the Land Trust and located adjacent to Libbey Beach County Park. Beach access, tidepools, trails, bird habitat.

Longview Seed Orchard. 38 acres inside Ebey's Reserve. Conifer seed orchard providing scenic open space, agricultural land and wildlife habitat. Now protected by Navy and Land Trust conservation easements.

Maxwelton Wetlands Preserve. 24 acres donated to the Land Trust by the Orach Corporation. Wildlife habitat, scenic vistas, wetlands and stream. Maxwelton watershed protection.

Mitchell Conservation Easement. 13 acres with 900 feet of shoreline at Polnell Point, protected by a conservation easement donated by Norma Mitchell and her family. Archaeological site, waterfront open space, wildlife habitat.

Moon Conservation Easement. 26 acres in Ebey's Reserve on central Whidbey protected by easement donated by John Moon. 16 acres of agricultural land and 10 acres of forest.

Naas Preserve. 33 acres, two-thirds of a mile of undeveloped coastline and remnant prairie in Ebey's Reserve on central Whidbey Island. One of the last 12 places in the world with a large colony of native golden paintbrush. Endangered plants, scenic vistas, public access and trails, wildlife habitat. Purchased by the Land Trust with private donations and government grants.

Putney Woods (Goss Lake). 600 acres northwest of Langley. Non-motorized recreational trails, mature forest, rare plant community, wildlife habitat and watershed protection. Transferred to Island County after a campaign led by the Land Trust, under the state Trust Land Transfer program.

Ryan Additon (Wilbert Trail). 7.3 acres adjacent to South Whidbey State Park, saved by a cooperative effort between a local grassroots organization, Save the Trees, and the Land Trust, State Parks and Island County.

Saratoga Woods. 118 acres northwest of Langley, saved in a cooperative effort between a grassroots group, Friends of Saratoga Woods, and the Land Trust. Owned by Island County, with a conservation easement held by the Land Trust, this property includes an old farmstead, extensive wetlands, second-growth forest, and trails.

Useless Bay Conservation Easement. 54 acres adjoining Deer Lagoon on south Whidbey Island. The Gabelein family worked with the Land Trust to develop a conservation easement that protects both working farmland and wildlife habitat.

Whidbey Institute Conservation Easement. 59 acres adjoining the Whidbey Institute on south Whidbey Island. The donated easement ensures the land remains in educational use and protects wildlife, scenic values and a natural forest community. Hiking trails provided.

Zimmerman Conservation Easement. 28 acres north of Clinton on South Whidbey Island. The donated easement preserves 28 acres owned by the Zimmerman and Raymond families, with forest, agricultural land, waterfront and wildlife habitat. The land is next to a popular bicycle and walking trail.

Naas Preserve includes two-thirds of a mile of undeveloped coastline and remnant prairie. © 2009 Mark Sheehan.

46   South Whidbey State Park and the Wilbert Trail are known for their remnant old-growth, including the 500-year-old "Ancient Cedar."

Wilbert Trail and South Whidbey State Park

A walk in the remnant old growth with forest ecologist, Elliott Menashe

Standing in the shadow of giant old-growth firs and cedars at South Whidbey State Park, Elliott Menashe remembers a story. It's about a woman who attended one of his classes on forest management.

"She was imperious – a real tough cookie," he says, shaking his head. He'd been telling the class about forest snags and all the reasons to leave them intact as wildlife habitat, but the woman was not buying it. "I've got a 60-foot snag that's about six feet thick," she said. "It's annoying me and I want it gone."

Menashe asked if it was a safety hazard. No. And was it full of woodpecker holes?

"Yeah, it's got those. But I want it gone."

"You just moved here, right?" he asked, then offered her a deal. "Leave it alone, and in a year if you don't change your mind, I will pay for its removal."

Elliott Menashe in a sea of sword ferns.

Juvenile Great Horned Owl

About a year later a package showed up in the mail. "It's a bottle of really good wine. Chocolates. And pictures of, you know, baby owls, eagles, osprey, herons, kingfishers – all these pictures. She said, 'If you hadn't stopped me I would never have known what I was doing. Thank you so much. I look around me now with different eyes.'"

The story illustrates an error Menashe sees often as principal of Greenbelt Consulting, *www.greenbeltconsulting.com*, a natural resources consulting firm. Newcomers often don't seek advice about living in harmony with nature. Arriving on the island from an urban or suburban setting of traditional lawns and landscaping, and with little previous contact with wildlife and woodland processes, their first impulse is to clear a big view, eradicate native vegetation and replace it with neat, manicured suburbia.

In the process they destroy all the best, most wondrous and magical reasons to live on the island.

Moss and ferns grow on a decomposing stump.

A good place to become immersed in those wonders is the mile-long Wilbert Trail, across Smuggler's Cove Road from the entrance to South Whidbey State Park. Parallel parking for several cars is available at the trailhead on a widened section of road shoulder about 0.4-mile feet north of the park entrance. It is marked with a crosswalk and a small sign identifying the Wilbert Trail.

Left: "The Ancient Cedar" is several hundred feet from the trailhead.

"This is not a true old-growth forest," Menashe clarifies. "It's a mature forest with old growth remnants." The distinction is important but takes nothing away from the impact. A few steps from the highway, hikers enter a sea of sword ferns. Several hundred feet later they come to a mammoth Western Red Cedar, next to a bench on which to sit and contemplate. "The Ancient Cedar" is estimated at 500 years old, but Menashe says it's probably not the oldest tree on this trail. Altogether, only about 1 to 5 percent of old growth forest remains in the Puget Sound Basin and Menashe says every bit of it is priceless and deserves to be saved.

Winter Wren © 2009 Craig Johnson

It is worthwhile to look up once in a while.

Left alone, the natural rotation of the island's forests would be 600 to 900 years. Historically, the forest was hit every few centuries by fires, volcanic eruptions and other cataclysms. Douglas firs, with their thick bark, often survived fires that killed thinner-barked species. "When the Europeans arrived in the 1800s this was a mature forest about 400 years old," he says. Douglas firs can grow up to 1,300 years, though it's uncommon, he says. Early loggers took the trees of high value that were easier to get. "The big trees we see today are the ones that weren't worth taking 150 years ago, and they're still healthy." Some already were several centuries old when the loggers passed them by.

It turns out the old, pre-industrial style of logging was healthier for the forest than today's clear-cutting, Menashe says. The pick-and-choose approach helped maintain a succession of age classes and a mix of species. Early loggers also left many dead, upright snags, decomposing stumps and fallen "nurse logs" that continued to provide wildlife habitat and nourishment. Five species of birds – mainly woodpeckers – are the primary excavators of these decaying leftovers. "If it weren't for them, 20 or 30 other wildlife species would have no homes."

In most harvesting of trees today, loggers strip the land bare so they can plant a new crop of Douglas fir. To germinate, Douglas fir requires exposed mineral soil and sunlight. But after the industry started germinating their seedlings in nurseries, the entire pretext for conventional clear-cutting went away.

"Loggers don't have to strip the land anymore, yet they want to because it's efficient for them," Menashe says. "But it's not cost-effective for society."

Planting many acres of one species, all of the same age, creates a monoculture that leads to forest health problems. Nature's system is far better, he says. A natural forest is a constantly shifting mosaic of multiple species, of many ages, growing side-by-side in ecological pockets.

Twin Flower

"Let's see how many species we have here," he says, looking around. "There's alder, cedar, hemlock, Douglas fir…uh, maple – aren't they exquisite? – and some Grand fir. And when we get to the wetter area we'll start seeing Sitka spruce. On south Whidbey, spruce is found only in a narrow band running from here to right around Bush Point."

Menashe carries a three-foot metal probe. He punches it easily into the forest floor nearly to the hilt. "That's duff," he says. "It's like a sponge and it protects the underlying soil from erosion."

The forest generates mulch to keep its floor healthy and rich. "Sword ferns protect the forest floor from erosion. They are the super plant for erosion control in the Pacific Northwest."

"In a native forest like this, with well-developed forest duff, 14 inches of rain can fall and less than one percent will run off as surface water." Menashe says forests are priceless in capturing rainfall and absorbing it into the earth so it can return to the aquifer from which most islanders draw their drinking water.

Deer ferns surround a clear pool in the wetland area.

Whidbey Island's Special Places

He points to a carpet of white-flowered ground cover growing amid the trees. "This is called Twin Flower. Now get a picture of this because this is really amazing. You don't see this in disturbed forests. It's evergreen and look how extensive it is. This stuff is really hard to get growing."

About 15 minutes into the walk, the forest begins to change. "Now here we are coming into the wetland," he says. "Look at this," punching his probe through a foot of humus and tree roots into flowing water underneath.

"The ground we are walking on is suspended over the water by a network of roots. If you jump in places the whole thing just goes 'whompeta, whompeta.'"

Running water emerges beside the trail into small pools that are crystal clear, having been filtered by the forest duff. "Look how clean the water is. It takes about 100 years for an inch of this wetland soil to form. This is just… the value of this is incalculable."

Twin Flower grows in a mound beside the trail.

The wetlands are extensive but surprisingly well concealed except by changes in the surrounding vegetation. Suddenly missing are the Douglas firs, which like their feet dry. The trailside here is characterized by cedars, hemlocks and Sitka spruce, and delicate deer ferns.

The Wilbert Trail is just one of several walks within South Whidbey State Park. The 250-acre parcel of woods, known as the Classic U Forest, was saved from cutting in 1978 by a grassroots citizen movement called Save the Trees. In 2006 the group sprang to action again to save an adjacent 7.3 acres near The Ancient Cedar. Working with Whidbey Camano Land Trust, the Island County Commissioners and Washington State Parks, they were successful and the additional acreage now is included within the state park.

The ancient trees of the Wilbert Trail have seen generations of humanity come and go, and will likely see generations more. They tower over mere humans, having lived here for centuries in perfect balance with the land.

It is well worth taking some time to reflect on that, in the spirit of true humility.

Mt. Rainier dominates the skyline on a clear day at Double Bluff Beach, just south of Freeland.

What's there: Walking, wading, picnicking, beach combing, off-leash dog area, bird watching.

To get there: From Highway 525 two miles east of Freeland, turn south on Double Bluff Road and drive two miles to road end at water's edge. This is a county park with parking for 20+ vehicles and access to two miles of public tideland to the west (only). Please respect privately-owned uplands and the private tidelands to the east.

Double Bluff Beach and Deer Lagoon

A closer look at the beach with biologist Sarah Schmidt

"Oh, look at that Killdeer. It's doing the broken-wing thing," Sarah Schmidt enthuses. The little bird flutters ahead on the sand, twisting its body and splaying its feathers as if injured. "It's trying to get our attention and lead us, which probably means we are close to its nest."

Like many who visit Double Bluff Beach winter or summer, Schmidt is noticing the details. Her attention is torn between the birds on the horizon and the tiny crab that just etched the scratchy trail at her feet. She's also listening – "What I'm hearing now are White-crowned Sparrows" – and scanning the tidal debris line for jetsam, or trash, which is surprisingly scarce.

A lone wind surfer stands at the water's edge and several parties of walkers with dogs head for the off-leash area, which extends west as far as the eye can see on this expanse of sand and surf. Already, several Bald Eagles have swooped low over the sand flats laid bare by a -3 tide.

Schmidt is peering through binoculars. "There are three herons in the shallows down there, and an eagle on the beach. It seems to be feeding on something. I wonder if the reason we see so many eagles here is because so much dead stuff washes up. This shoreline is exposed and gets a huge amount of debris coming up after storms," she says.

Killdeer doing broken-wing act.
© 2009 Craig Johnson

Sarah Schmidt

Large boulder, left behind by the retreating glacier 10,000 years ago, is encrusted with barnacles, mussels and other life.

age and left behind when the glacier retreated. "There is no source of these rocks locally and they're too big to be pushed by storms." She peers closely at the barnacles. "We've got some of the really big haystack barnacles… whooo, this one just moved. It's moving. That's so cool.

"I'm guessing one of the reasons we find all this life attached to the rock is because it's stable. Creatures can attach their eggs here. For the most part this rock is going to be under water and is protected. If they attached themselves to the smaller rocks they could get churned up a lot."

Rivulets of sand trickle from the steep bluff for which this beach is named. Near the crown, updrafts are whipping a shifting cloud of silt into the air. Coastal geologists call this a feeder bluff exceptional. It's a major, active source of eroding sediment to replenish sandy beaches such as this one and nearby Maxwelton Beach, which would otherwise be scoured down to rocky cobble by currents.

Schmidt is president of Whidbey Audubon Society. A biologist and bat enthusiast, she is also former head of the Washington State University Beach Watchers' program in Island County and co-author of the popular local guide, *Getting to the Water's Edge on Whidbey and Camano Islands.*

For many, this county park is South Whidbey Island's best kept secret, an unrivaled place to picnic, sunbathe, play in the sand, get away to think or exercise the dog. For Schmidt it is a precious natural place to view and appreciate geology and biology.

Twenty minutes down the beach, Schmidt pauses at a group of large boulders encrusted with large barnacles and tube worms. "These are glacial erratics," she explains, referring to the out-of-place rocks carried here during the last ice

This curious find is the egg collar of a Moon Snail.

Sand from the bluff helps create the perfect growing medium for offshore eelgrass, a key part of the marine food web for salmon, brant and other creatures. Once little appreciated, eelgrass today is highly prized and protected for its importance to shoreline life. Schmidt points out several strands of eelgrass snagged on the beach, which suggests that whole beds of the marine plant lie out of sight in the nearby shallows. The sandy substrate, nourished by the feeder bluff, is also favored by ghost shrimp, which attract migrating gray whales to scoop up mouthfuls of the bottom and sift out the shrimp. Eelgrass provides shelter for juvenile salmon and egg-laying habitat for Pacific Herring, one of the forage fish that salmon eat. Salmon attract not only recreational and commercial fishers but also orcas, the most magnificent marine mammals that reside in Puget Sound.

As rich with life as this beach is, Schmidt speaks even more reverently of the wetlands of Deer Lagoon, which share the Useless Bay shoreline with Double Bluff Beach but currently offer no adequate public access. "I'm thinking about the rich bird life I've seen at Deer Lagoon. If you go behind the spit on the east side of Deer Lagoon it is very tidal. When the tide is down you've got all kinds of birds – Dunlin and Western Sandpiper, and Black-bellied Plover, and some of the more migratory birds. And you come in on the west side and there are large numbers of ducks – scaup and wigeons and pintails and buffleheads, quite a range. You'll have many hundreds, if not thousands."

At the urging of Whidbey Audubon Society, the county several years ago recognized Deer Lagoon and Useless Bay as Habitats of Local Importance in their planning under the Growth Management Act. Deer Lagoon is also one of a handful of Important Bird Areas recognized by the Audubon Society in Western Washington.

Black-bellied Plover foraging at Deer Lagoon. © 2009 Craig Johnson

Sand erodes constantly from the high bluff, replenishing the beach and creating habitat for eelgrass, forage fish and other life.

Schmidt points out that as a native of New England, one of the joys of living in Puget Sound is how important its rich marine waters are to wintering birds. "If you're a bird watcher there's a lot more to see in the winter than summer," she says. Species that go away to Alaska or the boreal forest to nest in the spring come back in the winter. "I'm not sure I've ever lived anyplace where I was so excited as fall approaches because all these water birds start coming back."

With that in mind, what does Schmidt hope the public will realize when they visit Double Bluff Beach and others on the island?

"I hope we would all remember that the beach is the home of a lot of other creatures," Schmidt says. "When we're playing and exploring I hope we can do it with care so we don't disrupt their homes."

She walks on, deep in thought.

"I was just reading a book about Rachel Carson," Schmidt brings up. "The author of this particular book talked about how Carson was one of the propelling factors in the environmental movement that arose in the late 60s and 70s.

"Critics of the environmental movement sometimes say people treat it like a religion. The author was explaining there are some similarities, in that both are about ethics. People who are thoughtful about the environment have a real sense of living in an ethical way. Religion is about how we treat other people – how we live in relationship to other humans. Environmentalism is more about how we live in relationship with all the other living things on the Earth and see ourselves as part of the web of life rather than separate."

Schmidt believes that as people become more observant about what's happening in nature, they begin to place a greater value on each creature. "Beach Watchers is one organization that provides an opportunity for people to really take time to be on a beach, to look and see what's there.

Left: Beach bum, Sue Van Etten, spends some quality time with Rocky.

The beach shows the effects of wind and water currents in this view west toward Double Bluff.

The more we see all the things that are living here – like under these holes in the sand – the more we will realize we don't want to cover them up, for example with a pile of sand from a hole we've dug, and let them smother.

"We need to foster that sense of wonder throughout our lives, that awareness of what is around us, paying attention, discovering and appreciating, instead of getting too busy with everyday things and being oblivious."

It's a simple but profound thought, the kind of clear thinking that emerges on a good, long walk on the beach. Something about the wide expanse and high cliffs of Double Bluff Beach encourages those thoughts, whether walking alone, with a joyous dog, or just catching up with an old friend.

58   Langley, photographed from the air by Veronica von Allwörden, is surrounded by fields, forests and the waters of Saratoga Passage. © 2009 Veronica von Allwörden

Langley and the Gray Whales

Over and under with pilot, diver and photographer, Veronica von Allwörden

Snorkeling in front of her Langley home, Veronica von Allwörden was not expecting the big gray whale that suddenly surfaced about 50 feet ahead. "And then this other one surfaced between me and the first one. It was about 25 feet off and I just turned and swam the other way. That's too close for me. It's like a submarine coming up next to you."

The experience typifies the intimate nature of life in one of Puget Sound's most picturesque seaside villages. Everything is close, including the wildlife. "I love being able to walk into town," she says. "For me, of course, it's also having the beach, and the eagles, birds and deer. We can walk to a restaurant or movie, and we have the marina right here where we can put in the kayaks or go diving."

And even though von Allwörden and her husband, Eric, live in town, their home is nestled in a woodland setting near a bluff. When the wind blows, a forest dweller's thoughts turn to what could come down. "You don't garden when it's windy," she points out.

Veronica von Allwörden

Since moving to the shore several years ago, von Allwörden has grown more attuned to the daily changes in Saratoga Passage. She is increasingly engaged in whale research, community outreach and working to improve the health of Puget Sound. She gave a talk on gray whales at Langley's

Welcome the Whales Day. "More and more I'm involved with The Orca Network, and a lot of that is with the gray whales and the situation with ghost shrimp, on which they feed."

Von Allwörden already was used to being among fish. An avid diver, she volunteers twice a month at the Seattle Aquarium, doing research on octopi and six-gill sharks, and giving educational talks with an underwater microphone from inside a large viewing tank. But gray whales can be 50 feet long and weigh 35 tons. Swimming beside such a mammoth mammal is sobering. "It's pretty intense," she says.

On the day of her close encounter, von Allwörden had earlier noticed the gray whales feeding in front of her home and put on a wetsuit. "I had swum out quite a ways. The whales had gone over toward Camano Island, but then they circled back and that's when this whale surfaced and rolled over and started to feed."

She explained that the Marine Mammal Protection Act requires the public to keep a distance of at least 100 yards from protected species. "When I'm snorkeling and there are whales in the vicinity I'm very careful not to get too close. This just happened to be the whales' choice to get close to me."

Seven to 12 gray whales visit Saratoga Passage nearly every year during their spring migration to Alaska from calving grounds off the coast of Baja California. From March through early June they appear at various points along the shorelines of Whidbey and Camano islands, including the sandy shallows in front of Langley.

They come for ghost shrimp, which are plentiful in Saratoga Passage. The whales scoop up mouthfuls of the muddy bottom, leaving shallow depressions called "whale pits" in the process. They use their baleen to sift the shrimp from the substrate.

Left: Gray whales stir up the muddy bottom while scooping mouthfuls of ghost shrimp, a few miles from Langley. © 2009 Veronica von Allwörden

Painted Greenling lingers at the tire reef near Langley Marina. © 2009 Veronica von Allwörden

"Much of the ghost shrimp have been eradicated in the south sound," von Allwörden says. In many of those areas the state leases tidelands to the shellfish industry. Ghost shrimp generate a fine silt when they feed, which tends to smother other shellfish, so the industry applies pesticides to eliminate the ghost shrimp.

She rolls her eyes. "Right. Exactly. The pesticides are pretty ironic, given that we are trying to clean up Puget Sound."

But in Saratoga Passage and the waters near Langley, the whales find abundant shrimp to rebuild their energy reserves on the northward migration. "By the time they get here they have not eaten for four or five months. Every once in a while we have one starve to death, so you know they are just making it here. If a whale is new to the sound and goes down to the south sound, often it dies. It doesn't make it out."

Ghost shrimp like protected waters. "We have huge areas of ghost shrimp here, including a large area off Everett where the Snohomish River comes in."

In the spring, von Allwörden often observes gray whales from above while carrying out aerial photography assignments for her business, Sky & Sea Photography, *www.skyandseaphotography.com*. The unusual niche combines two of her great passions, and, like a lot of good ideas, came about partly by chance.

She had been perfecting her above-water photography for several years when, one day, she made a discovery while diving near Langley Marina. "In the mud I saw about that much yellow," she says, making a circle with her thumb and forefinger. "So I reached in and pulled out a dive camera. Since it had been covered with mud, it was protected from growth on the lens and didn't have any barnacles or anything. Yeah! So I took it home, opened it up and it was still dry. I replaced all the seals, put in new batteries and loaded up the film and it worked."

White and Orange-Tipped Nudibranch is a colorful resident of the tire reef near Langley Marina. © 2009 Veronica von Allwörden

That opened the door to a new world of underwater photography and led to better and better cameras. In the process she has built a large stock file of colorful underwater images. Many were taken at the tire reef, a structure used briefly as a breakwater near Langley Marina before it sank in a winter storm in the 1970s. "Now it's a large reef with anemones," von Allwörden says. "There are ling cod, perch, rockfish, octopus, and Dungeness and red rock crabs."

The same sheltered cove, which von Allwörden describes as a "bite" out of the shoreline, is not only popular with divers but is steeped in history. Langley was a fuel stop for the wood-burning pocket steamships of the Mosquito Fleet era, from the late 1800s to early 1900s. Jacob Anthes, the town's founder, had a thriving business selling cordwood to keep the ships' boilers going.

Left: A curious Lingcod approaches the camera at Langley tire reef. ©2009 Veronica von Allwörden

First Street in picturesque downtown Langley. © 2009 Veronica von Allwörden

It's a good reminder about fragility, beauty and quality of life. Whidbey Island's special places are special because many people care deeply, learn all they can, and live with respect for nature and the land.

Langley, like all of Whidbey Island, is a jewel in a million-dollar setting. It is surrounded by forests, blue waters, breathtaking views and snowcapped mountains. Gray whales and orcas still visit its shores. It's why those who are blessed to live in Langley and just about anywhere else on Whidbey Island pinch themselves every day to see if they're dreaming.

Below: Aerial view shows Cascade Avenue along the rim of the bluff, turning into First Street at top right.
© 2009 Veronica von Allwörden

In Langley, history and nature both remain close. They are two big reasons why many people feel a special affection for Langley, a strong sense-of-place.

From the air, von Allwörden sees the whole, how things are connected. On an island there is no escaping those connections and the consequences of what people do to the earth at their feet and water that surrounds them. From the air, "You can kind of peek into other people's worlds," she says. "There are people who have their own dumps! There's the house, then a little trail, and then the dump. You can see who's neat. Who's not. Who's got the car collection."

"We have a limited aquifer," she points out, noting that most island residents draw their drinking water from wells. So it really matters what they put into the ground. "We sit in the middle of Puget Sound. When you live on an island, everything affects everything else much more obviously than it might somewhere else."

Learn More

Many people are working to preserve the rural landscapes, natural habitat and rich cultural history of Whidbey Island. To learn more about the people in this book and some of the groups engaged in this work, please visit these websites.

- Admiralty Head Lighthouse, www.admiraltyhead.wsu.edu
- Greenbelt Consulting, Elliott Menashe, www.greenbeltconsulting.com
- Island County Shore Stewards, www.shorestewards.org
- Our Puget Sound Birds & Habitat, Craig & Joy Johnson, www.pugetsoundbackyardbirds.com
- Sky and Sea Photography, Veronica von Allworden, www.skyandseaphotography.com
- Sunnyside Cemetery, www.sunnysidecemetery.org
- The Orca Network, Howard Garrett & Susan Berta, www.orcanetwork.org
- Whidbey Audubon Society, www.whidbeyaudubon.org
- Whidbey Camano Land Trust, www.wclt.org
- Whidbey Environmental Action Network, www.whidbeyenvironment.org
- WSU Beach Watchers – Island County, www.beachwatchers.wsu.edu/island
- WSU Master Gardeners, www.island.wsu.edu/mastergardener/GBF